peace

30 DEVOTIONS ON
TRADING YOUR
ANXIETY FOR PEACE

LIFEWAY STUDENTS | DEVOTIONS FOR GIRLS

© 2020 LifeWay Press®

No part of this work may be reproduced or transmitted in any form or by any means, electronic or mechanical, including photocopying and recording, or by any information storage or retrieval system, except as may be expressly permitted in writing by the publisher. Requests for permission should be addressed in writing to LifeWay Press®, One LifeWay Plaza, Nashville, TN 37234.

ISBN 978-1-0877-4094-4
Item 005831346
Dewey Decimal Classification Number: 242
Subject Heading: DEVOTIONAL LITERATURE /
BIBLE STUDY AND TEACHING / GOD

Printed in the United States of America

Student Ministry Publishing
LifeWay Resources
One LifeWay Plaza
Nashville, Tennessee 37234

We believe that the Bible has God for its author; salvation for its end; and truth, without any mixture of error, for its matter and that all Scripture is totally true and trustworthy. To review LifeWay's doctrinal guideline, please visit www.lifeway.com/doctrinalguideline.

publishing team

Director, Student Ministry
Ben Trueblood

Manager, Student Ministry Publishing
John Paul Basham

Editorial Team Leader
Karen Daniel

Editor
Stephanie Cross

Graphic Designer
Kaitlin Redmond

table of contents

intro

What's your greatest fear? You might be afraid of something physical like spiders or having a bad hair day. Or maybe you're afraid of something a little less visible like rejection, gossip, or exclusion. Whatever your fears may be, have they ever caused you to experience heart-racing, palms-sweating, can't-form-a-coherent-thought anxiety?

If so, you're not alone. There's a lot going on in our world today, and it's completely understandable that you'd feel anxious. Sometimes our fears and worries threaten to overwhelm us. But God never intended for us to live wrapped up so tightly in worry, fear, and uncertainty that we feel like we can't breathe. No, the God who gave us breath intended for us to live full and courageous lives, characterized by His peace.

In this world broken by sin, our hearts cry out for God's peace. It's the balm our souls crave, and our God, who so faithfully loves and cares for us, didn't leave our cries unanswered. He sent His Son, Jesus, to die for us to have peace with Him. And then He sent the Holy Spirit to dwell within us and help us live in His peace every day.

Over the next 30 days, you'll dig into the truth of God's Word to answer three important questions about anxiety and the peace only God can give.

- How can my relationship with God help me fight anxiety?

- How can the church help those who struggle with anxiety?

- How do I set my heart and mind on God's peace?

You'll also find these additional resources to help you grow in the wisdom and strength to fight any anxiety that comes your way: Scripture memory coloring pages, encouraging quotes and helpful Scripture, an anxiety quiz and practical tips to fight anxiety, as well as resources for further study and action.

Girls, we pray that as you dive into these devotions, you'll see how God might be answering these questions in your life. And we encourage you to pray about how He might use you to help others answer these questions as well.

getting started

This devotional contains 30 days of content, broken down into sections that each answer a specific question related to peace. Each day is broken down into three elements—discover, delight, and display—to help you answer core questions related to Scripture.

discover

This section helps you examine the passage in light of who God is and determine what it says about your identity in light of that. Included here is the key passage and focus Scripture, along with illustrations and commentary to guide you as you study.

delight

In this section, you'll be challenged by questions and activities that help you see how God is alive and active in every detail of His Word and your life. You'll be guided to ask yourself what the passage means when it comes to your relationship with God.

display

Here's where you really take action. Display calls you to apply what you've learned from each day's study. At the end of the book, you'll find space to write out the challenges you accepted and how you fulfilled them.

prayer

Each day also includes a prayer activity in one of the three main sections.

Throughout the devotional, you'll also find extra articles and activities to help you connect with the topic personally, such as Scripture memory verses, additional resources, and quotes from leading Christian voices.

day 1

FIND GOD, FIND PEACE

discover|

READ

ROMANS 5:1-5.

Therefore, since we have been justified by faith,
we have peace with God through our Lord Jesus Christ.
—Romans 5:1

Throughout history, the people God called His own have rebelled again and again. God relentlessly and lovingly pursued them into foreign lands, out of slavery, through prophets and judges and kings—yet they still turned toward false gods and unholy ways of living.

Doing things their way did not bring them peace. What they needed was the truth—their sin was separating them from God. And the only way to get the peace they needed was through repentance and obedience.

The same is true for us. God has a plan to bring us peace through His son, Jesus. He sent Jesus to be the once-for-all, perfect sacrifice to forever atone for all of our sins—past, present, and future.

When we place our faith in Jesus for salvation, the Bible says we are justified and have peace with God (Rom. 5:1). Every barrier to our relationship with Him was wiped out through Jesus' blood on the cross.

Peace within ourselves and peace with others first begins when we have peace with God. As you will see throughout this devotional, a healthy relationship with God is foundational to being at peace and handling anxiety—no matter what comes your way.

delight |

When you're anxious or discouraged, where's the first place you look for peace? Why?

How does the truth of your rebellion and sin affect you? Explain.

How does the truth of God's love, pursuit, and gift of peace affect you? Explain.

display |

Since we're focusing on making peace with God today, take a minute to ask yourself: *Have I made peace with God?*

If you haven't, talk to your parents, small group leader, youth pastor, or an older, godly Christian. Ask them to get in touch with you one day this week to talk about what it means to make peace with God. Consider walking through this devotion with them.

Spend some time in prayer. If you have made peace with God, first thank Him for making peace possible through Jesus. Praise Him for the gift of Jesus' sacrifice on your behalf. Then, confess to God times when you've tried to find peace apart from Him.

day 2

GOD KEEPS HIS PROMISES

discover|

READ

JOSHUA 1:1-9.

"Haven't I commanded you: be strong and courageous? Do not be afraid or discouraged, for the LORD your God is with you wherever you go." —Joshua 1:9

To set the scene for today's passage, Moses—the Israelites' leader—had died. The thought of life without Moses's leadership must have frightened many, just as difficult circumstances may frighten God's people today.

Of all the people in Israel who'd followed Moses, Joshua probably felt the weight of Moses' death most deeply. Joshua had served as Moses' assistant, but now the leadership responsibility landed squarely on his shoulders.

Thankfully, this was part of God's plan all along. He wouldn't leave Joshua—or His people. He had promised them His presence and security. And He would deliver them into the land He had promised them, too.

Moses had been preparing Joshua to take over the leadership role. Beginning in Deuteronomy 31:3-8, he gave Joshua a bit of a pep talk, much like God did in today's verses. Both served to remind Joshua, and all of God's people, that He had not forgotten them or His promise to them.

Think about words or phrases a friend might use to encourage you to do something you're afraid of. Why do you think pep talks are effective in stressful, challenging, and frightening situations? Well, it's easy to get discouraged and anxious when all we can see are

---

changes and the weight of responsibility crashing down on us. This is why God encouraged Joshua first through Moses, then through His own voice.

In spite of the risks and challenges, God promises protection and success to those who courageously obey Him. Even if your circumstances change, God has not abandoned you. So, walk courageously into whatever He leads you to next.

delight |

God had asked the Israelites to enter a land filled with their enemies. On the surface, this seemed risky. What might God be calling you to do that seems risky?

How does knowing God keeps His promises give you peace when life is difficult?

display |

Look back at Joshua 1:6-9. List the specific attitudes necessary to obey God's call. Beside each one, list one way you can cultivate that specific attitude in your own life.

> Think of a time when you've been afraid to go where God has called you, but you obeyed anyway. Thank God for being with you, no matter where you go. Then, praise Him for giving you the confidence to walk boldly into any situation.

day 3

COMFORT AND CALM

discover|

"Don't let your heart be troubled. Believe in God; believe also in me."
—John 14:1

This belief, or trust, Jesus called for in His disciples was deeply relational. He had been walking with them for a while, but now He called them to continue His ministry—even though He was no longer going to be on earth with them.

Jesus was leaving them and returning to the Father. It makes sense that the disciples would be a little "troubled." Jesus knew this news would be upsetting, as would the events of the coming days. He knew His disciples would feel anxious and uncertain about what to do and even about all He'd taught them while He was with them. Still, He said, "Trust God. Trust me."

In pointing their attention to God and Himself, Jesus reminded His followers that it might have seemed like the world held all the power—and it might have even seemed that their victorious King wasn't so victorious—but God would have the final say.

The storms of life will hit us no matter how strong our faith is. We wouldn't be human if we didn't experience disappointment, anxiety, and fear along with contentment, peace, and courage. Because of Jesus, our hearts can rest rather than be troubled. Through Him, we experience the comfort and calm of God's peace, even as the world around us seems to be going crazy.

delight |

Think about a time when you trusted Jesus through a difficult circumstance. How did He bring you peace during that time?

When anxiety or fear feel overwhelming, how does John 14:1-7 teach you to trust that God is who He says He is and that it's okay to not be "troubled"?

How does this passage help you experience comfort and calm, even circumstances are out of your control?

> Think about the situations in your life that are beyond your control. Ask God to give you the confidence to face these situations without fear or anxiety about the outcome. Thank Him for the tender way He cares for you.

display |

Take a minute and think about your life. Using the notes pages or a journal, write about a few things that are "troubling" you right now. Then, take your favorite color marker and write the words *Trust God* in big letter over the list as a reminder to trust God above all.

It can be difficult to "give over" a situation to God, since it's such a mental and spiritual battle. So, talk with a godly, trustworthy person. Ask this person to check in with you at the end of the week. Give them permission to ask, "How did you trust God with _____ this week?"

day 4

TRUE PEACE

discover |

Peace I leave with you. My peace I give to you. I do not give to you as the world gives. Don't let your heart be troubled or fearful. —John 14:27

The world will give you a lot of tips for handling anxiety. You can have a therapy session online, even through chat. You can download an app that teaches deep breathing and relaxation techniques. Maybe you listen to a soothing sounds playlist or workout. Or maybe you even do a deep dive into funny videos. Our society offers many tools to cope with anxiety.

But only Jesus can *give* you peace.

Yes, taking deep breaths slows your heart rate and allows you to think clearer. Yes, talking to a counselor when you feel overwhelmed is healthy. And yes, learning to relax instead of focusing on the negative situation you're facing is good too. Although these tools and strategies are incredibly helpful, they can't you true, lasting peace on their own.

It's the source of our peace that makes the difference.

In today's passage, Jesus was about to go to the cross. As we discussed yesterday, He would no longer be walking the earth with His disciples. Their entire world was about to change. But Jesus promised something more.

In the midst of this whirlwind of events, Jesus taught His disciples about real peace—peace that comes from God and is different from worldly peace. Because God alone is sovereign and in control, He alone can provide true peace.

delight |

How is the peace Jesus offers different from the peace the world offers?

How can you respond when people try to tell you worldly peace is like the peace that God gives?

List some things that are acting as roadblocks to peace for you right now. Take a few minutes and write ways God's peace can help you face each one.

Ask God to help you seek His peace, even when life feels overwhelming.

display |

If you're feeling anxious and overwhelmed today, try one of these strategies for focusing your heart and mind on Jesus, the One who gives us peace.

- Throughout the rest of the month, memorize John 14:27. Whenever you feel anxious or afraid, say this verse aloud and pray that God would remind you of His presence in your life.

- Set aside anything that might distract you. Create a playlist of your favorite worship songs—the ones that really encourage you. Spend a few minutes listening to this playlist today.

day 5

VICTORIOUS

---

discover |

READ
JOHN 16:31-33.

"I have told you these things so that in me you may have peace. You will have suffering in this world. Be courageous! I have conquered the world."
—John 16:33

Again, Jesus was trying to prepare His disciples for life on earth after He was no longer physically with them. Jesus made it clear that, although God was sending the Holy Spirit to dwell with believers, life wouldn't magically become easy. In fact, Jesus actually promised His disciples they would suffer. He even used words like *scattered* and *alone* to describe their immediate future. That's encouraging, right?

But Jesus didn't leave His disciples confused or concerned about this; He pointed them back to God, then to Himself. First He told them He wouldn't be alone because the Father would be with Him. Then, He said the same would be true for them: "You'll find peace in me. Yes, even when you suffer."

Jesus knew His disciples would feel scared and uncertain with all that would take place. He wanted them to be absolutely confident, even calm. Jesus focused on the victory He knew God would bring. He knew the Father's plan. He trusted His Father. He knew that He had already conquered the world. The plan was set in motion. The enemy couldn't stop it.

Jesus knew that what was coming would affect them all deeply. But He also knew He was already victorious. And that was where He wanted His disciples to gather their courage.

Since Jesus has given us peace and overcome the world, then that truth should make a difference in how we live our daily lives. We should live victoriously with faith in Jesus, our Victor.

Take a moment and thank God for Jesus who overcame victoriously, and that, through salvation, we can do the same.

delight |

Think about a few instances in your life when you felt victorious. Why did they make you feel victorious?

How have you experienced the peace Jesus promised when you were facing something difficult?

How will you actively choose to trust Jesus to work in and through those difficult situations? List three ideas. Ask God to empower you with His Spirit so you will trust Him in all things.

-

-

-

display |

Today, challenge yourself not to play the "What if … " game. Every single day, we face difficult situations, and God asks us to do difficult things. But our God is trustworthy, and we already have victory in Him. So, when you're tempted today to wonder "What if … " in the face of your trials, write out on an index card *But God* _____. On the other side of the card, list at least one passage of Scripture that shows why you can trust God in this situation. Consider writing out your memory verse: John 14:27.

day 6

THE GOD WHO COMFORTS

discover |

READ
1 KINGS 19:1-9.

Then the angel of the Lord returned for a second time and touched him. He said,
"Get up and eat, or the journey will be too much for you."
—1 Kings 19:7

On Mount Carmel, God used Elijah to show the prophets of Baal, and all of Israel, that He was still in charge. Elijah killed all of the prophets of Baal, and when Israel's Queen Jezebel found out, she vowed to kill him (vv. 1-2). Despite knowing God's power and having just seen it firsthand, Elijah ran in fear. He even despaired to the point that he wished for death.

Elijah quickly moved from an extreme high to an extreme low. But Elijah's fear wasn't really about a wicked queen threatening to kill him. When he was threatened, Elijah forgot the truth of God's power and doubted God's ability to protect and provide for him. When we face uncertainty, doubt, and pain, it's easy to respond just like Elijah—to run in fear.

Elijah felt super anxious because of what he was going through. Despite Elijah's forgetfulness and despair, God comforted him by providing bread and water, delivered by an angel. This response is true to God's nature. We can trust God to give us strength and comfort, even when our anxiety seems overwhelming.

delight |

What does God's provision for Elijah tell you about God's character?

When have you seen God provide for you or someone you know in times of extreme anxiety, doubt, or despair?

How does God's care for Elijah give you peace for the times you feel afraid or anxious?

display |

Take a minute to think about all the ways God has provided for you recently. Even think about what He's given you that you didn't know you needed. Focus on this truth: God is greater than your anxiety and fear. Now, ask God to show you how He responds to our despair with love and attention.

> Spend some time thanking God for all the ways He has provided for you.

Anxiety can make you feel like you're drowning and alone. But you aren't alone. Think of one person you can trust to give you godly advice and encourage you. Set a time to share with that person any anxiety you may be carrying. Ask them to commit to praying for you and walking through this season with you.

Ask yourself: *What helps me when I feel anxious*? Now, consider how that might help someone else you know who experiences anxiety, too. Write out your "help" on an index card and give it to that person this week to encourage them.

day 7

NOT ALONE

discover |

READ
1 KINGS 19:9B-18.

He replied, "I have been very zealous for the Lord God of Armies, but the Israelites have abandoned your covenant, torn down your altars, and killed your prophets with the sword. I alone am left, and they are looking for me to take my life." —1 Kings 19:10

When Elijah called on the Lord in front of the prophets of Baal, God showed up. He sent fire from heaven that "consumed the burnt offering, the wood, the stones, and the dust, and it licked up the water that was in the trench" (1 Kings 18:38). The people saw and declared that the Lord is God, but with Jezebel threatening to end Elijah's life—Elijah was understandably afraid.

In today's passage, Elijah wasn't just afraid—he also felt completely alone in His fear. But God met him there, where he was, hiding in a cave, and asked, "What are you doing here, Elijah?" Elijah's answer revealed more than a fear of death; it showed a fear of being alone. So, God spoke specifically to that fear. He said, "I will leave seven thousand in Israel—every knee that has not bowed to Baal and every mouth that has not kissed him" (v. 18).

We see this theme of a remnant, or group set apart as faithful followers of God, throughout Scripture. No other human being ran to the mountain with Elijah, so Elijah assumed he was alone. But God challenged Elijah's assumptions, and He does the same for us as He consistently reveals Himself to us through His faithful followers. He reminds us that we are not alone.

> Thank God for always being present with you, especially when you feel alone, afraid, and anxious. Thank Him for giving you the encouragement of other believers in your life, too.

delight |

Think about the patterns that led to Elijah's discouragement. What similar things do you see in your own life?

Note the way God responded to Elijah's negativity. How does He often respond to your negativity?

Focus on verses 11-13. Notice how God unexpectedly revealed His presence. How does God sometimes reveal His presence to you in unexpected ways?

display |

Jot down the names of a few believers who have strengthened you in your walk with Christ, and thank God for them. Choose at least one name from the list, and write that person a thank-you note, telling them what their encouragement has meant to you. If you want to get creative, consider making your own card with a personalized message.

Now, think of a friend who might need some encouragement. Send her a quick text or a hand-written note of encouragement. You could also consider talking with and praying for her.

day 8

A SOFT WHISPER

discover|

READ

1 KINGS 19:1-18.

Then he said, "Go out and stand on the mountain in the LORD's presence."
—1 Kings 19:11

Have you ever come back from a camp or retreat with a passion to live boldly as a disciple of Christ, but then life suddenly became more difficult? Maybe you felt vulnerable and attacked. The prophet Elijah experienced something very similar after defeating the prophets of Baal at Mt. Carmel.

John called Satan "a liar," really emphasizing this truth by calling him "the father of lies" (John 8:44). But what part do the enemy's lies play in Elijah's story? Well, Elijah thought He was alone—abandoned by God and without any other person who was also faithful to God. But Elijah was wrong.

When Elijah ran, God showed up. Elijah was not so alone or vulnerable anymore. And God made His presence known to a very vulnerable Elijah in an incredibly gentle way. Through a "soft whisper," God reminded Elijah that He—the Creator of the universe—was still very present with Elijah (v. 12). He saw Elijah and heard his cries about feeling so alone. So, God reminded Elijah that He was with him and had called other believers to be with him too.

Our participation in God's story can deepen spiritual moments, which can sometimes make us vulnerable to the enemy. Just like He did for Elijah, God constantly reminds us that He is here with us and that He has placed others in our lives to be with us as we live out His calling to build His kingdom.

delight |

What are some ways God has reminded you that He is with you, even in difficult circumstances?

How does God's gentleness encourage or comfort you when you're feeling defeated? Explain.

display |

Elijah felt alone in his faith, but he wasn't (v. 18). There will be moments in your faith journey when you feel alone. If you're not already, get involved with a local church and invest in the lives of other Christians now. When dark times come, these friends can remind you about God's presence, character, and plan.

This may also be a good time to find an accountability partner. An accountability partner doesn't have to be your best friend, but should be a godly girl or woman you can trust. This will be a girl you can lean on during the good and the bad, who will love you enough to tell you the truth and help you see when you might not be pursuing God's best.

> Thank God for the people who hold you accountable to pursuing Him and His best for you. If you don't have this type of person in your life, pray that God would bring someone along to help hold you accountable.

day 9

GRACE FOR THE HUMBLE

discover|

READ
1 KINGS 21:17-29.

"Have you seen how Ahab has humbled himself before me? I will not bring the disaster during his lifetime, because he has humbled himself before me. I will bring the disaster on his house during his son's lifetime." —1 Kings 21:29

In 1 Kings 21:1-16, King Ahab asked Naboth to sell his vineyard. Naboth refused, and Ahab went home pouting. So Jezebel, Ahab's wife, plotted to take the vineyard from Naboth. She sent a letter—along with some false witnesses—in Ahab's name, accusing Naboth of treason and ordering the city's elders to stone him to death. Naboth was killed, and Ahab got the vineyard. And that's exactly where the Lord met Ahab and changed his story.

When Elijah first showed up, Ahab wasn't happy about it. Then Elijah delivered the bad news. But instead of threatening, attacking, or mocking Elijah, Ahab repented (v. 27). As wicked as Ahab was, when confronted with the truth of his sin, he responded in humility. God wants us to respond the same way.

Sometimes, our own sin causes our anxiety. Maybe we know we have done something wrong or have a habit we'd like to keep hidden, and we lose sleep over it or worry about getting caught. Honestly—as weird as it is to say—if we would follow Ahab's example of repentance, we could let go of some anxiety.

We have to humble ourselves and admit where we have gone wrong. We need to confess to God when we have been keeping secret sin and living in ways that are not pleasing to Him. Then, we can rest in the grace God offers us and release the burden of trying to carry the weight of our sin.

delight |

Consider how God responded to Ahab's humility and repentance. How does that response display God's grace and mercy?

How does a humble attitude indicate a heart-change?

What are some ways God's grace and mercy has changed you?

How has God's peace and presence allowed you to do difficult things?

> Remember, God disciplines those He loves (Heb. 12:6). Take a minute to praise God for how He is shaping you to be more like Jesus.

display |

It's easy to write people off. We think, *Oh, they'll never change.* But God shows us over and over again that He is in the business of changing lives. So, think about this: Who have you written off? Now, ask yourself a difficult question: *Is God asking me to extend forgiveness to this person*? Think about reaching out to this person today.

Maybe you're the person you think is too messed up for God to use. Be honest with God about what you're feeling and thinking. Admit your sin and seek His forgiveness. Ask Him to make His grace and mercy very real to you.

CONFIDENCE AND PEACE

discover|

READ
2 KINGS 2:1-14.

[Elisha] picked up the mantle that had fallen off Elijah, and went back and stood on the bank of the Jordan. He took the mantle Elijah had dropped, and he struck the water. "Where is the LORD God of Elijah?" he asked. He struck the water himself, and it parted to the right and the left, and Elisha crossed over.
—2 Kings 2:13-14

As we know, Elijah experienced many ups and downs in His life, but God had given him someone to support his ministry: Elisha.

Prophets were in constant opposition and conflict with many of the people of Israel. So, it's safe to say Elisha may have had some anxieties about what would happen when God took his mentor into heaven. And it probably didn't help that people kept reminding Elisha about Elijah's impending departure.

In today's passage, Elisha watched his mentor be taken into heaven in "a chariot of fire with horses of fire" (v. 11). He watched until Elijah was no longer in sight, then turned back to the Jordan—and to his people. Imagine the uncertainty and the weight of responsibility Elisha felt.

But God is good, and just like He met Elijah in the cave, He met Elisha before he even crossed the Jordan to return to his people.

Before he took his first steps into ministry without Elijah, God confirmed Elisha's call to succeed Elijah. God did this by allowing Elisha to use Elijah's mantle to part the waters exactly the same way his mentor had as they walked across the river earlier.

God confirmed Elisha's calling and calmed his fears before sending him forward on mission. When God confirms that we are right where He wants us to be, we can walk forward with confidence and peace, knowing God is guiding our steps.

delight |

When have you seen evidence of God's presence in your own life?

The Holy Spirit dwells within believers; He is always with us. How does this comfort you and give you confidence?

How does Elisha's story encourage you to trust God—especially when facing the unknown?

display |

Ask yourself: *What am I afraid to do?* Sometimes, speaking aloud or writing out the truth can help us start on the right path. So take a minute to say your fear aloud and write it out.

Spend some time in prayer, asking God to show you how to move forward in faith and with His peace rather than fear.

Peace

"PEACE
I leave with you.
MY PEACE
I give to you.
I DO NOT GIVE
TO YOU AS THE
WORLD GIVES.
Don't let your heart be
TROUBLED OR
FEARFUL."

JOHN 14:27

day 11

PEACEMAKERS

discover|

READ
MATTHEW 5:9.

"Blessed are the peacemakers, for they will be called sons of God."
—Matthew 5:9

There are many kinds of peace—military, relational, environmental—but the kind of peace described in Matthew 5:9 is spiritual. If you're at peace spiritually, then you're at peace with God. And the only way to be at peace with God is to reconciled to Him through the forgiveness of sins.

Finding peace and rest from our anxiety begins with peace with God. Although only the Holy Spirit can give a person peace with God, peacemakers can show the way and help people understand how to be reconciled to God.

Peacemakers are actively involved in bringing reconciliation between those in conflict. They love God and others and want to share the gospel, bringing peace to all who receive it.

But peacemakers don't just help others learn to be at peace with God and one another, they also support us when we face those trials Jesus mentioned. They remind us that He has overcome the world. They don't promise absolute peace or the end to our battles, but they do fight for us in prayer and with encouragement. They pursue God above all and peace with others as much as is possible (Rom. 12:18)—and they encourage us to do the same.

True peace, the kind peacemakers help us see and the kind we're called to help others find, is a sense of wholeness and harmony that only comes through a relationship with Jesus.

Pursuing this peace and helping others find it is one of our greatest callings as children of God.

> Pray that God would give you the wisdom and courage to share His peace with others.

delight |

Where has God called you to be a peacemaker? Explain.

Describe some ways Jesus made peace during His earthly ministry. Which of these things can we do to be peacemakers today?

display |

If you're a Christian, you have received God's peace. But your pursuit of peace doesn't end there—you are now called to share the Source of your peace with the rest of the world. In a journal or notes page, respond to the following:

- How is God making me more like Him in this season?
- What are some ways He has gifted me to share the gospel?

  (Are you a good writer, teacher, encourager, or friend? Explain.)
- Who do you find difficult to love, make peace with, or tell about Jesus? Journal a prayer asking God to soften your heart toward this person and give you opportunities to share the gospel with them.

day 12

SHOW UP

discover

READ
LUKE 10:25-37.

"Which of these three do you think proved to be a neighbor to the man who fell into the hands of the robbers?" "The one who showed mercy to him," he said. Then Jesus told him, "Go and do the same." —Luke 10:36-37

The religious people of Jesus' day wanted to know who exactly qualified as their neighbor. Jesus answered the question with a parable—the one we know as "the Good Samaritan." The basic idea? Our neighbor could be anyone, so God calls us to love all people as we love ourselves.

That sounds tough, right? Thankfully, God doesn't leave us to do any guesswork about how to love our neighbors. In fact, in the parable Jesus told, the Good Samaritan shows us several ways to love others well.

- Be compassionate.
- Stop, and be present.
- Go to the person who's hurting.
- Bandage wounds.
- Provide with care.

The Bible specifically says the Good Samaritan "took care of him" (Luke 10:34). We are called to care for one another—physically, mentally, emotionally, and spiritually.

We aren't called to beat each other up with words like, "Don't be anxious, just pray more" or "You just need to trust God" or "Maybe if your faith was stronger, you wouldn't be anxious."

No.

We show up. We stop what we're doing. We listen. We provide with tenderness and compassion. We do not pass by and ignore one another's pain. We show with our words and actions that we care.

We are present, we are real, and we prayerfully take these needs before the Lord on behalf of those who cannot do so themselves.

delight |

How has Jesus taken care of you, shown you compassion, and provided an example for you to do the same?

What ways are you struggling—spiritually, physically, emotionally—today? How does Jesus bring you peace even here?

Who has been there for you, no matter what? How have they compassionately pointed you toward Jesus when you're hurting?

display |

Ask God to reveal to you three people you who are struggling. Now, list their names and one way you can help each of them this week. As you look for ways to help, continue to pray for each person on your list.

-
-
-

day 13

VULNERABILITY REQUIRED

discover |

READ
GALATIANS 6:1-2.

Carry one another's burdens; in this way you will fulfill the law of Christ.
—Galatians 6:2

As we talked about yesterday, loving one another and pursuing peace together means caring for one another. Paul describes this as carrying one another's burdens. We love as Jesus called us to when we love this way.

One of the key themes of Galatians is the freedom that grace brings to believers. It is freedom *from* sin and the freedom *to* truly love others. In chapter 6, Paul applied that freedom to our relationships. Grace frees us from selfishness so we can bear each others' burdens and minister with pure motives.

But loving this way requires vulnerability—whether we're the ones sharing or carrying. It's tough to open up to others when we're struggling. It's tough to ask for help. But both are absolutely necessary. We were not made to go through life alone; God designed us for community.

When we share our struggles, the church isn't there to judge us, but encourages us toward God in gentle, loving, kind, and healthy ways.

Anxiety isn't necessarily a sin, either. It can cause us to slip into sinful behaviors or make us doubt and fear and do other things that aren't God-honoring. But, instead of treating anxiety like a wrong, think of it as a sign that helps you recognize something else is wrong.

In other words, anxiety isn't necessarily the sin but may point you to the sin or a deeper brokenness in you or the world around you. Sometimes, our anxiety is out of our control. But our anxiety is never, ever out of God's control. And we can face our anxiety courageously in the loving arms of our Christian community.

When you're feeling anxious, don't retreat, reach out. Reach out to others in your church to come alongside you, to pray with you, to encourage you. Reach out to God, placing your anxiety squarely on His shoulders—He promises to care for you and to carry your burdens (Matt. 11:28-30; 1 Pet. 5:7).

delight |

What are some ways you can be more present for someone who's hurting?

Opening up to others is scary, but others can't care for you well if you don't let them in. How can you be more open when you struggle?

> Pray that God would help you to not only carry others burdens, but also open up about your own, letting other believers pray for, encourage, and support you.

display |

Sometimes it's actually easier to want to help others than it is to seek help for ourselves. But think about your life right now. What's heavy in your life? What seems like too much for you to carry? What are you anxious, depressed, nervous, or stressed about? Write out a few different things.

Spend some time praying, asking God to bring to mind someone you can trust to be vulnerable with. It might feel a bit uncomfortable, but take the next step. Reach out to that person, share your story, and ask for their support.

day 14

WHAT NOT TO DO

discover

READ
JOB 42.

"After the Lord had finished speaking to Job, he said to Eliphaz the Temanite, "I am angry with you and your two friends, for you have not spoken the truth about me, as my servant Job has." —Job 42:7

Sometimes, we understand why difficult things happen, and feel some sense of peace. But, there are times when we experience tough things and have no idea why. And when we ask God, we're met with silence. So, then, we're stressed, anxious, and confused. If anyone ever could understand this feeling, it was Job.

Job was righteous in God's eyes and was rich by all standards. Although he had done nothing wrong, Job lost everything and experienced incredible emotional and physical pain.

We can learn a lot about how to help others handle difficult situations from the Book of Job. We can also learn what not to do. Neither Job's friends nor his wife were very helpful. His wife told him to "Curse God and die!" (2:9), and his friends didn't do any better. Rather than listening to Job and sitting with him in His pain, they basically told him he must have done something wrong and angered God.

But Job didn't believe that, and in the end, God confronted Job's friends for speaking falsely about Him. No matter what anyone said, Job both refused to admit guilt and refused to accuse God. Job's response to His trial wasn't perfect, but it was an example to his friends: You can ask God questions about why something is happening and yet continue to praise and trust Him.

Like Job, when we do this well in our less-than-peaceful moments, we can change the way people around us view God. We can encourage them to trust Him and His character rather than questioning Him when things go wrong.

Being at peace with God in difficult circumstances isn't just for us; it helps others learn how to respond, too. Faith encourages faith. So, keep trusting. God is still good, even when life is not.

delight |

You can't experience God's peace without trusting Him. When has it been difficult for you to trust God?

Think about some confusing and difficult situations in your life. How have you learned to find your peace in God, even when life is tough?

display |

Examine your heart. How do you respond to difficulties? Do you respond in faith, like Job, or in frustration like his wife and friends? Choose one of the options below to commit to responding in faith, even when you don't understand what God is doing.

- Write a poem or song about God's goodness. Keep the words with you as a reminder when you feel discouraged.
- Paint, draw, or use an app to artistically display the words, "Faith encourages faith." Or Make a short video, sharing how God has ultimately brought good to you out of a tough situation. Post this on social media or send it to a friend who's walking through a tough time.

Ask God to help you respond to tough times like Job did. Pray that your faith remains strong even when life is difficult. Also, ask God to help you be a friend who is willing to stay with others when they have difficult days.

day 15

REJOICE TOGETHER

discover|

READ
LUKE 1:57-58.

Then her neighbors and relatives heard that the Lord had shown her his great mercy, and they rejoiced with her. —Luke 1:58

> Take a couple minutes to be still. Think about the word *rejoice* and what it means to you. Consider the things God has done and who He is to you.

The word *rejoice* isn't one we hear often, but it's an important theme throughout the Bible and in the Christian community. When bad things happen, we mourn together and support one another. When good things happen and the Lord fulfills His promises, we rejoice (or celebrate) together.

The word *rejoice* most commonly means to feel a deep sense of joy. That's exactly what happened with Elizabeth—she, her family, and her neighbors felt a deep sense of joy together as they celebrated together the birth of her son.

Think about her situation. She and Zechariah were "well along in years" (Luke 1:7), and she had been unable to have children most of her life. But God had promised them a child, and not just any child, but one who would prepare the way for Jesus—God's own Son (vv. 13-17).

Consider the emotions the couple must have felt—they'd wanted a child for so long and had been unable to have one. Finally, God answered their prayers, and Elizabeth gave birth to John.

Elizabeth and Zechariah weren't alone when they rejoiced—their community surrounded them. The same people who had likely prayed over the couple, asking God to give them a child, and then prayed for the baby's safe arrival, now surround them in celebration.

The church isn't just there to support us when we're anxious or scared or upset—the church is there to celebrate with us when God's good promises are fulfilled. We're together on the tough days, but we're together on the good days, too.

delight |

Think about your own life. How have your friends and church community celebrated with you when God answered prayers or fulfilled promises in your life?

Think about the people around you. How do you see God working in their lives, and how can you celebrate with them this week?

display |

Look back at the definition of *rejoice*. Grab three sticky notes and write out three prayers God has answered for you recently. Place these where you can see them each day this week. Keep the sticky notes and a pen nearby, and write out one way you rejoiced over or celebrated each of these answers this month, placing the note with the answer it celebrates.

When God moves in our lives, it affects the people around us. Consider sharing with your friends, small group, or even your student ministry how God is working in your life, showing His faithfulness and answering prayers. Not only will this encourage people to rejoice with you, but it will also encourage others to make requests of their own to God.

quotes

To fight our fears, we will look at God's sovereignty and love and watch our fears dissipate as we apply God's Word to our lives.[1]
Trillia Newbell

The presence of anxiety is unavoidable, but the prison of anxiety is optional.[2]
Max Lucado

Peace isn't a quiet life, peace is a quiet soul. Peace is the gift of Jesus through the work of Jesus that we can have no matter what's going on in our living rooms or our inboxes or our Facebook feeds. The loudest of lives can't overwhelm the quiet that comes from Christ.[3]
Scarlet Hiltibidal

Some of the greatest gifts in life come from the scary places.[4]
Priscilla Shirer

When we're alone and vulnerable, we feel afraid. When we're together and vulnerable, we become brave. A brave group of vulnerable people acting together in faith is not easily overcome by anxiety and stress.[5]
Rebekah Lyons

I may be here for a day, for a year, or even for five years, but at the end of it all, this depression and anxiety is not eternal. What is eternal is my soul, and it's going to be bomb one day with Jesus. I have to set my hope on what is going to come eventually in eternity.[6]
Jackie Hill Perry

Because of your faith, you can trust in the goodness of God above. In that trust, anxiety vanishes; care flees as clouds before the sunshine. What a great sense of freedom we have in turning over all of our cares and concerns to God.[7]
Dr. Gardner C. Taylor

scripture for when you're anxious

When you're anxious or worried, it can be difficult to focus on anything other than the issue itself. But if you've tried this, you know it's true: You can't change what you're focusing on by telling yourself to stop thinking about it; this only makes you think about it more. So, how do you break the cycle of anxious thoughts swirling around in your brain? How do you relax your anxious heart?

Cognitive Behavioral Therapy (CBT) often uses thought-replacement to treat anxiety. Basically, you practice replacing negative thoughts with positive ones.[8] And in Philippians 4:8-9, Paul tells believers to do the same: Focus on godly things and God's peace will be with you. That sounds simple, right?

We know the constant battle with our thoughts—especially anxious ones—is anything but easy. Thankfully, God has equipped us with His Word and His Spirit to fight. And that is exactly what we're going to do. You may find verses more fitting to your unique struggles and anxieties, but here are a few fears and verses to help you fight them.

For the days when you're worried about the future.

Therefore don't worry about tomorrow, because tomorrow will worry about itself. Each day has enough trouble of its own.
Matthew 6:34

For the days when you feel like you can't take another step and your anxiety is overwhelming.

I am able to do all things through him who strengthens me.
Philippians 4:13

For the days when you wonder what can chase away your fears.
There is no fear in love; instead, perfect love drives out fear, because fear involves punishment. So the one who fears is not complete in love.
1 John 4:18

For the days that seem to shatter your faith and confidence.
The result of righteousness will be peace; the effect of righteousness will be quiet confidence forever.
Isaiah 32:17

day 16

FAITHFUL GOD

██████████ ————————

discover|

READ

LUKE 1:67-80.

Blessed is the Lord, the God of Israel, because he has visited and provided redemption for his people. He has raised up a horn of salvation for us in the house of his servant David.
—Luke 1: 68-69

Take a look at the characteristics listed in this passage.

- God provided redemption.

- He made a way for salvation.

- He fulfilled the promises He spoke through His prophets.

- He rescued from enemies.

- He gave mercy.

- He remembered His covenant with His people.

- He removes fear.

- He is holy and righteous.

- He surrounds with His presence.

Here Zechariah described just how amazing God is and how faithful He is to His people. Let's be clear: These aren't just messages for the early church or for those who happened to be in Zechariah and Elizabeth's home. These words—these promises—are from God to you as well.

While so many things fill us with fear, anxiety and dread, God has not changed. God promised us salvation. He promised us a Prince of Peace (Isa. 9:6). He promised to make a way for us—not just for us to come to know Him but for us to have a full and abundant life in Him (John 10:10).

He knew this life on earth would be difficult, even with His promises. Even with Jesus. Even with the Holy Spirit. He knew we would be tempted to worry. He clearly promised that we would have troubles, but He also just as clearly declared that we would have salvation because He has already overcome (John 16:33).

Because our God is faithful, anxiety and fear do not have the final word. And His Spirit seals us with His promise (Eph. 1:13).

delight |

Are you waiting for God to fulfill any promises in your life? Explain.

Using the notes pages at the end of this devotional, journal about one way you've seen God's compassion and mercy in your own life.

Take a minute to thank God for all the ways He has been compassionate, merciful, and faithful to you. You can write out your prayer or say it aloud.

display |

Choose a verse that is meaningful to you that speaks about God's faithfulness, create an artistic display, and then share the verse on social media along with a "caption" of how God has been faithful to you lately. If you don't use social media, find another way to share this verse and "caption."

day 17

WITHOUT FEAR

discover|

READ
LUKE 1:67-80

*He has dealt mercifully with our ancestors and remembered his holy covenant—
the oath that he swore to our father Abraham, to grant that we, having been
rescued from the hand of our enemies, would serve him without fear in holiness
and righteousness in his presence all our days.*
—Luke 1:72-75

The Jews pictured salvation as rescue from political enemies, but
God's salvation is about being free *from* sin and being free *to* serve
Him without hindrance or fear. Without Jesus, you are a slave to sin.
But with Jesus, you have the One who conquered sin on your side.
And He has the power to help you overcome sin.

In this passage, we see some key truths about God: He is merciful,
He remembers His covenant, He rescues us, and He allows us into
His presence. Then, we see some ways to serve Him: with boldness,
in holiness, and in righteousness.

We don't have to be afraid of the past because we have been
rescued from it. Who we were is a part of our story, but so is
Jesus. Paul even said those who are in Christ are new creations
(2 Cor. 5:17). And through the power of the Holy Spirit, we can walk
confidently in this new life (and future) God has given to us.

Because of God's faithfulness; Jesus' life, death, and resurrection;
and the Holy Spirit who lives within us—we don't have to be afraid
or worry about anything. This is the beauty of the gospel. Our God,
who calls us to boldly serve Him without fear, gives us the power to
overcome that fear and walk in peace and confidence as we fulfill
His calling on our lives.

delight |

Use the following questions to evaluate your life and guide your prayer time today.

- Ask Jesus to help you with any sins you feel powerless to overcome.

- Thank Jesus for what He has done to free you from sin and allow you to serve God without hindrance.

- What fears do you have about the future? Does the fact that God has a plan for your life fill you with fear or confidence? Ask God to give you the confidence to follow Him without fear.

display |

When we are stuck in sin, we sometimes become afraid of how God will react if we're honest with Him about that sin. He already knows. Be honest, confess your sin, and seek His forgiveness.

Then, take it a step further. Part of true biblical community is confession (Jas. 5:16). This is different from confessing your sins to God for forgiveness. It's good to confess your struggles to another believer who will not only hold you accountable to walk in holiness, but who will also encourage you as you continue your faith walk. Think about who this might be for you—maybe the girl you reached out to on Day 8—and share with her what's on your heart.

Finish each of the following sentences by filling in ways you can change your thinking and/or behaviors to serve God better.

- *I will serve God with boldness by ...*

- *I will serve God in holiness by ...*

- *I will serve God in righteousness by ...*

day 18

EVIDENCE

---

discover |

READ
GALATIANS 5:19-26.

Now those who belong to Christ Jesus have crucified the flesh with its passions and desires.
—Galatians 5:24

Knowing Jesus wrecks our lives in the best way possible. Thankfully, He doesn't leave us to figure out how to live godly lives on our own. When Jesus returned to heaven to be with the Father, God sent the Holy Spirit to dwell with believers. So, as soon as you trust in Jesus for salvation, you receive the Holy Spirit. He dwells within you, changing you from the inside out, and helping you live life God's way.

When the Holy Spirit is in control of our lives, sin no longer defines us. Instead, we are characterized by the fruit of the Spirit. The fruit of the Spirit include: "love, joy, peace, patience, kindness, goodness, faithfulness, gentleness, and self-control" (Gal. 5:22-23).

These traits are evidence of God working in our lives.

Experiencing anxiety and worry doesn't mean you're a bad Christian or living in sin. But, just like we should no longer live characterized by the "works of the flesh" (vv.19-21), our lives should also not be characterized by fear, anxiety, or worry. Our characteristics are the attributes that set us apart and tell who (and whose) we are.

Those who belong to Christ should generally have attributes that set us apart as His. So even when we do worry, our overall attitude, and the place we come back to, is ultimately absolute trust in God. Although we may experience anxiety, fear, or worry, God calls us to be characterized by Him and by hope, faith, and trust that He is who He says He is.

Our lives speak a loud testimony to those around us. What a great story we could tell if, even in moments of fear and anxiety, we consistently point to our loving Savior and the glorious truth of who He is and what He has done for us.

delight |

How does following the Spirit in your daily life bring you peace and joy?

What are some ways walking in the fruit of the Spirit has changed your life?

Are you trying to cultivate the fruit of the Spirit in your life by your own power? If so, confess that to Jesus, asking Him to help you rest in the Holy Spirit's power to grow and strengthen you for His service.

display |

Place a check mark by any of the following "works of the flesh" you struggle with. Confess these things to God and ask Him to help you walk in obedience.

- Gossip
- Pride
- Jealousy
- Anger

- Selfishness
- Lust
- _____
- _____

Now, think about the fruit of the Spirit. Prayerfully consider which are the most difficult for you to live out. Then ask God how you can live out each one today. Be sensitive to the Spirit's leading and consider how God might be calling you to demonstrate one of these traits to someone specific. If He is, commit to doing so the first chance you get.

day 19

REJOICE

■■■■

discover |

READ
PHILIPPIANS 4:4-7.

Rejoice in the Lord always. I will say it again: Rejoice! —Philippians 4:4

> **Are there things troubling you today? Take a minute and ask God to help you have joy in the midst of those struggles. Let His Word bring comfort to you as you dig into today's devotion.**

Paul experienced life-threatening trouble many times throughout his life. Yet, through all of it, he never seemed to take his focus off of making Jesus known. Take a look at the instructions Paul gave in this passage.

- Rejoice.

- Be gracious to everyone.

- Don't worry, pray instead.

- Ask God for what you need.

Graciousness can also be translated as gentleness. It isn't always easy to be gracious or gentle with others, especially when you're frustrated, anxious, or upset. But Paul makes a point to say that our graciousness should be known to everyone. Or, as he put it in his letter to the Romans, "If possible, as far as it depends on you, live at peace with everyone" (5:8).

God calls us to seek peace with Him and with others. When we do this, He guards our hearts with His peace. And our appropriate response, as Paul encouraged, is to rejoice in Him.

Believers only find complete joy, gentleness, and the peace to not be anxious in God (Gal. 5:22-23). This kind of gracious joy is not a human trait, but evidence of the Spirit at work within us.

delight |

When life is troubling, how do you find peace?

What might change in your life if your first step was taking your troubles to God?

No matter what is going on in life, we always have reasons to rejoice. Take a minute to think about all the reasons you have to rejoice. List a few here.

display |

Because of God, we can rejoice no matter what. Look back at the list you made of reasons you have to rejoice.

Write out a prayer to God, praising Him for who He is, for sending Jesus, and for the many ways He has taken care of you.

Grab four index cards and write out each of the instructions Paul gave in this passage. Make these cards as pretty as you like, fold them in half, and keep them with you. When you feel anxious, open one of these cards and take a minute to do what it says.

am i anxious?

Quick note: Answering these questions doesn't equal an anxiety disorder diagnosis; it's a tool to help you better understand your personal anxiety level. Think about your life over the last month and respond on a scale of 0-3 of how often you've experienced the following. Indicate your response by highlighting the number that best represents your response. Then, calculate and record your total in the blank.

0 = Not at all
1 = Sometimes
2 = Over half the time
3 = Almost every day

1 My thoughts race and I struggle to concentrate.

    0   1   2   3

2 I obsessively compare myself with others, wondering how I measure up against their efforts, successes, and so on.

    0   1   2   3

3 I feel nervous or edgy but don't know why.

    0   1   2   3

4 I can't seem to control my thoughts, and I'm in a constant state of worry.

    0   1   2   3

5 I'm restless; I have difficulty relaxing and sleeping.

    0   1   2   3

6 It's not difficult for me to become annoyed or irritated.

    0   1   2   3

7 When I attempt to focus on or accomplish something important, I feel (circle the emotions that apply to you): afraid, angry, helpless, guilty, ashamed, or disappointed.

    0   1   2   3

8 When I think about _____, I feel dizzy, experience nausea, and have headaches and muscle tension.

    0   1   2   3

Total: _____

10 and under: Your anxiety level is pretty low.
11-15: Your anxiety level is moderate.
Above 15 indicates severe anxiety.[8]

what can i do if i am anxious?

If you find yourself in a situation where you're feeling anxious, here are six tips to help you remain calm.

---

1 Try a brain dump. It's tough to think clearly when your brain feels scrambled. Grab a blank piece of paper, and write out as much of what's on your mind as possible. There's no specific format—make it as creative or simple as you want.

2 Do deep breathing exercises. Breathe in for four counts and out for six. The exhale is actually the part that calms us; that's why we do a few more counts there. Breathe in through your nose and out through your mouth.

3 Talk to your parents, a trusted Christian mentor, student pastor, or pastor. Find a godly person you're comfortable talking to and share your fears and anxieties with them. Sometimes, speaking something aloud (and sharing with trusted others) can help calm our anxious hearts.

4 Try journaling. Write about whatever anxiety you feel. Consider a pocket-sized journal that you can carry with you or an app on your phone so you can write whenever you begin feeling anxious.

5 Do a countdown. Mentally or verbally list five things you can see, four things you hear, three things you can touch, two things you smell, and one thing you can taste in that moment. This helps ground you in reality and step outside the overwhelming circumstance.

6 Meditate on Scripture. On p. 39, we provide some suggested Scripture to focus on when you're feeling anxious. But you don't have to stick to these verses. Think about all you've studied in God's Word, and this devotional, and choose a verse that helps you focus on His peace rather than the chaos around you.

Note: If you experience severe anxiety, you can take these steps to relieve symptoms; however, the best approach would be to seek out a professional Christian counselor.

day 20

WHAT IF?

discover |

READ
MATTHEW 6:25-34.

"But seek first the kingdom of God and his righteousness, and all these things will be provided for you."
—Matthew 6:33

In a fallen, sinful world, it's easy to think our lives have no meaning. And for Christians, it's tempting to consider this life as something we just have to get through until we get to spend eternity with Jesus. But God's intent for our lives tells us otherwise.

God has a purpose for each and every person on earth. And it's not for us to live in fear and anxiety, but to live in His perfect peace being at peace with Him, ourselves, and others. Even when we have dark days and life just seems like the worst—God still has a purpose and a plan for us.

Let's take a look at some of the assurances Jesus gave in this passage.

- Your life is more than what you eat or what you wear.

- God takes care of every living thing, even the birds. You're worth so much more than they are. He'll take care of you.

- You can't add anything to your life by worrying.

- God clothes the grass in color, which withers and dies away quickly. He will clothe you, His child—His eternal and beloved creation—too. And He wants to give you what's best.

- Don't worry; God knows what you need. We have enough to focus on today; relax and rest in God's care for what comes tomorrow.

These aren't assurances from just anyone, either—they came straight from Jesus. If you're stuck in the land of "what ifs" and worried about the future, know you're not alone. But also know this: God was aware of your need before you were. He has always provided and will always take care of you.

delight |

Consider your life: What do you lack?

What are you worried about for the future—whether it's tomorrow or ten years from now?

How do Jesus' words in this passage provide peace and comfort for your worries and fears?

display |

Look at the assurances listed in today's devotion. Highlight the one(s) most difficult for you to trust. In a journal or on a notes page, write out why trusting this truth is difficult. Then, ask God to help you trust in His promises.

Write out today's focus verse on an index card. Carry it with you, and any time you touch it, read it.

> Pray, asking God to help you focus on Him and seek His kingdom first. Ask Him to help you be a light to others who might be anxious or fearful of the future, encouraging them to pursue a deeper relationship with Him.

day 21

FAITH & HOPE

discover|

READ
HEBREWS 11.

Now faith is the reality of what is hoped for,
the proof of what is not seen.
—Hebrews 11:1

As you begin your time with God, think about all the ways we exercise faith on a daily basis. Have you ever stopped to consider what the words *faith* and *hope* actually mean? Simply put: Faith is belief and trust in something or someone (in this case, God), while hope is confidently waiting for something you want to happen.

If we look at those definitions in light of Scripture, how do things change? Let's plug these definitions into Hebrews 11:1 and see how that helps our understanding.

> Now [belief and trust in God] is the reality of what [we confidently wait for], the proof of what is not seen.

Faith is not about the strength of our belief, but the reality of the object of our faith. Christ's deity and sacrifice on the cross are the reality in which we place our faith. The promises He made to His followers are the source of our hope.

The rest of Hebrews 11 goes on to name many Old Testament believers who placed their faith in the reality of Christ by believing that He would come as promised. Like us, they did not get to see Christ in the flesh, but their faith was rooted in the reality of who He is, the hope of His salvation, and God's promises. In many ways, our faith is very similar to that of the patriarchs and prophets in the Old Testament.

Our faith in Him is our hope for the future. And because we know God keeps His promises, we can trust Him, living in obedience to Him without fear of what's ahead.

delight |

When you reflect on your walk with Christ, you may not often think of terms like reality or proof, but have you ever stopped to think about the fact that God is who He is whether we believe in Him or not? Write out some evidence that proves the reality of God's existence.

What proof do you have in your own life that Christ has made you new?

display |

If you were asked to explain the faith and hope to someone who doesn't know God, what would you say? Record a 30 to 60 second clip on your phone with your answer.

Look over the evidence you wrote out about God's existence. Then, look over the proofs you listed that Christ has made you new. Sometimes, sharing proofs from our own lives can help those who are struggling in their faith or have not trusted Jesus as Savior. Think about those around you. Who might need to hear the evidence or proof from your life?

Spend some time praying for God to soften that person's heart to hear His truth. Then, ask God to give you the opportunity and the words to share with them.

day 22

WHEN TO START

discover|

READ
MATTHEW 7:23-29

"Everyone who hears these words of mine and acts on them will be like a wise man who built his house on the rock." —Matthew 7:24

We've talked a lot about walking through life with anxiety and how having peace with God helps us experience peace in general, but when should we start seeking God's peace? When we feel afraid? When a difficult situation arises? When someone speaks unkindly to us? When what we'd been dreading actually happens? Or, maybe, should we start seeking God's peace before that?

The best time to seek God's peace is before the first sign of a problem. When we do this, we'll be ready when problems do come.

In this parable, Jesus tells us that the person who hears His words and acts on them is like the man who built his house on the rock. The rock stands for Jesus Himself. When you build your life on Jesus, you can experience peace, even on difficult days and in the darkest circumstances.

But, when you build your life on anything other than Jesus, and things fall apart—so do you. Anything we build our lives on other than Christ—relationships, family, money, popularity, followers—is sand. Sand won't hold up in a storm; it won't bring us the peace we so desperately need on the hard days. The world tells us we can build our lives on anything we want and stand tall in our own strength; that if we're strong, we'll have our peace. But that just isn't true.

Yes, people who build their lives on Jesus will still experience tough times. But, Jesus not only prepares us for the tough times, His peace also keeps us going and encourages us during those times. People who build on Him won't fall apart because we can give our worries to God, and He will fill us with His peace.

delight |

As you pray today, list some difficult things God prepared you for and brought you through. Thank God for helping you to walk through those tough times with His help.

List out any stressful situations you're currently facing. How have your reactions to stressful situations changed since you started this devotional?

display |

We build our lives on many things other than Christ. Highlight the one you're most tempted to build your life on (or write it out, if it isn't listed).

- relationships
- family
- money
- popularity

- followers
- academics
- sports
- _____

Take a few minutes to work on one of your memory verses or sing a praise song like "Build My Life" by Pat Barrett to focus your heart on Jesus. Commit to building your life on Him.

Picture in your mind someone who lives at peace even during tough times. Today, reach out to that person and ask when they could talk or get together. When you do, ask questions and watch how they find God's peace even in difficult situations. Consider building a relationship with this person, allowing them to mentor you in walking in God's peace at all times.

day 23

WHERE IS JESUS?

discover |

READ
MATTHEW 8:23-27.

He said to them, "Why are you afraid, you of little faith?" Then he got up and rebuked the winds and the sea, and there was a great calm. —Matthew 8:26

How do you keep your mind steady on God's peace, even when everything around you is falling apart? It's important to know you won't do this perfectly. Think about Jesus' disciples in this story. They went to Him, panicked, and woke Him up, saying, "We're going to die!" That sounds like a fun way to wake up, right?

What did Jesus say when He woke up? He rebuked them for not having faith. If we think we'd react similarly in the disciples' situation, then this rebuke can sting a little. When we're anxious, the last thing we want to hear is that we just need to have more faith. At this point in Jesus' relationship with His disciples, they'd seen Him work many miracles; they'd seen signs that pointed to His identity as God's Son and His power.

The very Son of God was right beside them in the storm.

But the disciples were scared, and when we're scared, it can be difficult to think straight. Even when we have a relationship with Jesus, sometimes we forget how loving, powerful, and protective He is. We may feel like He's sleeping, just like Jesus was on this boat. But again, just like in the boat with His disciples, He is aware of what is going on in our lives at all times.

When we feel tossed around and tired, God still asks us to trust, to have faith that we won't drown, even if we come out on the other side more than a little shaken.

No matter how great the fear or anxiety caused from the storms in your life may be, God is greater. And we have to remember, the very Son of God walks beside us in our storms too.

delight |

Are you living in peace, knowing He is in control, even during the out-of-control situations you're facing? What might be keeping you from peace?

How has God brought you peace and comfort during difficult circumstances?

display |

Although our minds often become overwhelmed when life is difficult, here are a few things we can do to stay at peace.

- Read the Bible.

- Pray.

- Memorize Scripture.

- Spend time with other believers who will listen, encourage, and love us.

- Go to church.

- Sing worship songs.

Highlight one of these that will help you focus on God's peace and commit to taking action when you feel anxious.

day 24

PEACE DURING CHAOS

discover

READ

MATTHEW 14:22-33.

Immediately Jesus spoke to them. "Have courage! It is I. Don't be afraid."
—Matthew 14:27

As we saw yesterday, sometimes Jesus calms the storm immediately when we call out to Him. But sometimes, Jesus teaches us to have peace during the storm.

It isn't enough to briefly look to Jesus during in a difficult situation and ask for help. We need to focus on Him during every part of it. When we look away from Jesus and focus on the storm, we begin to sink.

The Bible says the disciple's boat was once again being "battered by waves" (v. 25). As if that wasn't enough, they saw Jesus walking toward them on the water and they were filled with fear. Instead of being frustrated or immediately calling them out for their lack of faith, Jesus responded compassionately.

The ever-impulsive Peter spoke up first. While it might seem like Peter's statement revealed a lack of faith, that's not necessarily true. Instead, Peter's words showed a small faith, a growing confidence that Jesus was who He claimed to be. And an increasing belief that the he would be able to do incredible things when he trusted Jesus.

Jesus didn't rebuke Peter when he asked the question, got out of the boat, or began walking toward Him. Jesus didn't rebuke Peter when he began to sink. No, first, Jesus reached out His hand and saved Peter. Then, Jesus asked why Peter doubted.

Notice that only when they got back into the boat did the storm stop. Just like Jesus didn't stop Peter before he started to sink, He didn't stop the storm right away either. Jesus allowed His disciples to struggle, yes, but He brought them comfort, encouragement, and rescue, right there in the middle of it all.

Jesus may choose to calm the storm right away, like He did in yesterday's passage. But He might also let us experience the storm, allowing us to learn to trust in His presence and power and growing our faith.

delight |

Think of a tough time when you let a "storm" overwhelm you and take your focus off of Jesus. How did your perspective, and even the situation itself, change when you removed your focus from God?

What did you learn from that difficult season?

Spend a few minutes focusing on God. Until we can have peace with God in the quiet, still times, it will be difficult to have peace with Him during the chaotic, tough times. Ask God to help you be still and focus on Him more each day. Thank God for giving you His peace in the midst of the storm.

display |

Our faith, testimony, and relationship with God are strengthened when we learn to focus on Christ and experience His peace during times of crisis, instead of just expecting Him to fix the crisis. On a notes page, list some ways you can choose to focus on Christ, even when life is chaotic.

Our faith is also strengthened when we hear of what God has done for others in the midst of their storms. Ask God to guide you as you consider who might need to hear your story. Then, reach out to those people and share your own experiences of finding peace by focusing on God during a difficult time in your life.

day 25

HOW CAN I CONFRONT FEAR?

---

discover|

READ

PSALM 56:1-13.

When I am afraid, I will trust in you. —Psalm 56:3

We live in an evil world. The Bible even warns us that Satan prowls like a lion, looking for those he can devour (1 Pet. 5:8). But God says we should remain alert and levelheaded. Think about the anxiety we could avoid if we were paying attention and clear-minded enough to be more in control of our choices.

David knew difficult days. When he wrote Psalm 56, the Philistines had captured him. Instead of blaming God, David asked God for three things: to be gracious to him (v. 1), "to bring down the nations" (v. 7), and to put his tears in a bottle (v. 8). The rest of the Psalm, David spent praising God, affirming his trust in God over and over.

While David praised God because of who God is, praising God is also good for us. Not only were we made for it, but it also reminds us of who God is, what He has done for us in the past, and what He has promised to do for us in the future.

You may read David's words and wish you had the confidence to believe like he did, saying, "in God I trust; I will not be afraid. What can mere humans do to me?" (v. 4). It can be really difficult to set aside our fears and trust God, even when we know who He is and what He's done for us. Truly, fully trusting in God takes practice. David had lots of practice, and as you walk in faith throughout your life, you'll have the opportunity to practice trusting God too.

The only way to truly confront our fear is to trust in God fully.

---

delight |

How will you practice trusting God today?

Think about your own life and difficult situations in the past. How has speaking out what you know to be true about God and affirming your trust in God grown your trust in Him?

When have you faced something you were really afraid of and recognized that God was the One to bring you through it? Take a second to thank Him for walking with you in trials.

display |

Say Psalm 56:3 three times out loud. Memorizing and speaking Scripture aloud can be a powerful weapon against fear. The next time you feel anxious, say this verse aloud and focus on how good and powerful God is.

Spend a few minutes writing your own Psalm of praise, affirming your trust in God. Make it specific to your own life and current circumstances. Then, read back through your words, offering them as a prayer of praise and trust to God.

Worrying drains our energy, and the truth is that a lot of the things we worry about never even happen. List a few of the things you're worried about, then write out what it would look like to trust God in each of these circumstances.

day 26

YES, BUT ...

discover|

READ
NUMBERS 13:27-33; 14:9.

"Don't rebel against the LORD, and don't be afraid of the people of the land, for we will devour them. Their protection has been removed from them, and the LORD is with us. Don't be afraid of them!" —Numbers 14:9

Earlier in Numbers 13, God had commanded Moses to send a group of men to scout out the land of Canaan—which God was giving to the Israelites. The men obediently went into the land, but what they saw there terrified them. Yes, there was milk and honey as promised, but their enemies waited there too.

Caleb, one of the scouts, believed God and believed they could "certainly conquer it" (v. 30). But the rest of the people—except Joshua—were hesitant, to say the least.

They said, "Yes, Moses, the land is exactly as God described it, flowing with milk and honey. But we can't possibly attack because these people are stronger."

Basically, they knew this was the land God had promised to them, but they were afraid of what they saw there. And so, they began to make excuses—and it's tempting for us to respond to challenges the same way.

The way we respond to challenges can reveal what's in our hearts. If we don't want to do something, we typically see all the things that could go wrong and all the reasons we shouldn't try. But when we do want to do something, we see all the ways it can go right; we see possibilities instead of impossibilities.

But look at Caleb's words in Numbers 14:9. He saw the situation differently. Because the Lord was with them, they could do anything! Rather than saying "Yes, but…" Caleb reminded the people that their only right response was "Yes, because…"

You can say "Yes" to what God has called you to do, even in the face of fear, because He is with you and you can trust Him.

delight |

When you face something difficult, are you tempted to see the challenge as an enemy or opportunity? Explain.

Look at Caleb's response. How was it different from the others'? How does it encourage you to respond to challenging circumstances?

display |

Pray, asking God to help you see every challenge through His eyes. Is there something God has asked you to do that you've responded to with a timid, "No"? Ask God for the courage to say yes and to trust Him. Thank Him for being a God you can trust, and a God who is with you always.

In the coming days, if God gives you a chance trust Him with something that is challenging, say yes to Him. Don't worry about what might happen, be confident in the One who called you.

Try hand lettering the words *Yes, because* on an index card. Carry the card in your pocket, purse, or backpack. Anytime you begin to say "Yes, but" to something God calls you to do, pull out this card. Let it serve as a reminder of all the reasons you have to say yes instead.

day 27

CHASING FEAR

discover|

READ
1 SAMUEL 17:20-26,45-50.

"Then all the world will know that Israel has a God, and this whole assembly will know that it is not by sword or by spear that the LORD saves, for the battle is the LORD's. He will hand you over to us."
—1 Samuel 17:46-47

Initially, David wasn't involved in the battle at all—he was home, watching his father's sheep. But David's father had sent him to the battlefield with food for his brothers and their commander and to check on his brothers' wellbeing.

When he arrived, the army was marching out in battle formation, only to be sent running by the appearance of Goliath—the same Philistine warrior who had taunted them for 40 days. While all the soldiers went running, David essentially said, "Who is this Philistine man, and how dare he defy God" (v. 26)?

David didn't respond like the rest of the Israelite army. He was filled with righteous anger that someone would speak out against his God. While he was an Israelite, David wasn't just defending the people, his ultimate desire was to defend the Lord. No one could defy God like that and be allowed to stand, so David took action.

David's love for God, and his desire to see God feared and respected as He deserved, made him run toward his enemy and fight rather than run away and hide. David could chase down his enemy, knowing the Lord was the one truly fighting the battle.

You can do the same. Whatever you're afraid of, you can trust that God is with you. You won't face one single day alone as God's child. And You will never, ever face the enemy alone either.

delight |

How does God's presence in your life give you the confidence and strength to face your fears?

What's your initial response when someone misuses God's name or speaks negatively about Him?

What can you learn about responding to people who speak out against God from the way David responded to Goliath?

display |

David's courage and confidence came from his love for the Lord. Think of what you're facing today or what's going on in the world. How does your relationship with God give you the courage to speak boldly and defend His name? How does God strengthen you to chase down your fears?

Pray that God would help you to believe more in Him than your fear. Think of a few specific situations where you've felt like God has been asking you to speak up, to defend His name. Yet, you've been silent for fear of what people would do to you or say about you. Prayerfully consider how you might speak up in that situation the next time you have an opportunity.

day 28

discover |

READ
2 TIMOTHY 1:3-12.

For God has not given us a spirit of fear,
but one of power, love, and sound judgment. —2 Timothy 1:7

What's the first thing that pops into your mind when you hear the word *fear*? Most definitions mention negative feelings or emotions.

Think of it this way: The opposite of fear is _____.

By taking a look at what Paul said to Timothy, we see that the opposite of fear is: power, love, and sound judgment. Let's break these down a little more.

Power. The word *power* in this verse isn't just referring to physical strength. Rather, this power is spiritual, referring specifically to the power of the Holy Spirit at work within believers.

Love. In 1 John 4:18, we see that "There is no fear in love; instead, perfect love drives out fear." Many people who have been hurt in earthly relationships are afraid to love. This can cause them to withdraw from people rather than ministering in love. But God has given us His perfect, unconditional love, available to all even though some are cautious about receiving it.

Sound judgment. Having sound judgment means having wisdom and self-control. A person with sound judgment is steady and stands firm in their beliefs. Those who don't have sound judgment are always changing their values and beliefs for specific situations.

We know that God is the One who gives us a spirit of power, love, and sound judgment. The enemy is the one who gives us the opposite: fear. He wants to trap us in fear so we will be powerless, unloving, and have no direction, wisdom, or self-control in life. Next time you feel afraid, remember that fear is not from God.

Reach out to God, and ask Him to help you overcome your fear with His power, love, and sound judgment.

delight |

Fear comes from the enemy, but God gives us His Spirit to overcome it. How does this encourage you as you face difficult circumstances today?

How do you see God's Spirit at work in your life, even in the details?

How does the Holy Spirit help you have peace in situations big and small?

display |

Think about what you've felt God calling you to do lately. What fear have you felt? How can you use the power, love, and sound judgment God has given you to step out in obedience today? What is He asking you to do, and what one step can you take right now to step into His call?

Maybe you aren't struggling with fear and anxiety in your own life right now, but you know someone who is. Take a minute to write a note to that person, encouraging them to walk in the spirit God has given them.

day 29

TRUST GOD

discover |

READ
ISAIAH 26:1-4; PSALM 23

You will keep the mind that is dependent on you in perfect peace, for it is trusting in you. —Isaiah 26:3

You will keep the mind that is dependent on you in perfect peace, for it is trusting in you. —Isaiah 26:3

If someone tells you, "Don't think about an Apple," what immediately pops into your mind? An apple, right? To train our minds to think differently, we can't just tell ourselves not to think about something. Instead, we have to focus on something else.

So, if we want to set our minds on God rather than our anxiety, we take a positive stance. We don't tell ourselves not to think about anxiety-inducing situations; instead, we think about God. We think about the times He brought us peace and calm in the past. We think of His faithfulness, His love for us, His grace, His mercy.

This permissive, not restrictive, behavior is what begins to change us.

C. S. Lewis said, "Relying on God has to begin all over again every day as if nothing had yet been done."[9] Simply put: If you want to focus your heart and mind on God's peace, then you have to set your heart and mind on God Himself—every single day.

In Psalm 23, David provided a good example of praising God for fulfilling his needs. He affirmed that because the Lord was the One who led and guided him—his Shepherd—he knew he would have what he needed (v. 1).

Shifting your own thoughts toward praise and peace—no matter what—means you remember what God has done and what He has promised. Remember who He is. And praise Him for it all, even the days of darkness when He's the only light you see.

delight |

Look back at Psalm 23. Take a minute to complete the following statements, describing when and how God has done each of these things for you.

- *God provided quiet for me*

- *God renewed my life*

- *God led me*

- *God was present with me*

- *God gave me comfort*

- *God provided*

- *God blessed me*

- *God was good to me*

- *God pursued me*

- *God was present with me*

display |

You can also set your mind on God's peace by memorizing Scripture. Consider starting with the verses on pages 26-27 and 72-73.

Write each of the ways David proclaims his trust in God on individual index cards. Fold them up and place them in a jar. Each day, pull one index card from the jar and praise God for the way He has done that for you. For example, if you pull "God provides quiet," then praise Him for how He has provided quiet for you that day. Then fold the card and return it to the jar. Make this a daily practice so you build the habit of praising God for all things.

day 30

TWO WAYS OF PEACE

---

discover|

READ
PHILIPPIANS 4:6-9.

And the peace of God, which surpasses all understanding, will guard your hearts and minds in Christ Jesus.
—Philippians 4:7

Paul wrote this letter to the Philippians from prison. The Philippian believers were clearly worried about what would happen to him—and to them. Paul wasn't worried, though, and he wrote to encourage them to experience the same kind of peace in their relationship with Jesus.

The world says peace is found in the absence of conflict or in positive thinking, but this passage says that true peace is only found in trusting that God is in control.

Paul approaches peace two ways: how to have peace in the middle of difficult circumstances and how to create an environment of peace.

To have peace when life is tough, Paul instructed believers not to worry, but to pray, taking all of our worries straight to God. In the phrase, "peace of God," the word *peace* comes from a Greek word that also means "rest."[10] Paul did not envision a situation in which circumstances had changed or the problem was taken away. Instead, he emphasized that God's peace is rest—even in the middle of chaos.

Paul also suggested that creating an environment of peace starts with the way we think. So, he told believers exactly what to dwell on, including things that are: true, honorable, just, pure, lovely, commendable, morally excellent, or praiseworthy.

Then, he took it a step further and basically told them: Follow my instructions and the instruction of the other apostles. For us today, this means doing what God has outlined for us in His Word. When we walk in obedience to God, we will have God's peace—even if things around us seem to be falling apart.

delight |

How have you seen God's peace—even in personal conflict, stress, or struggles—over the last 30 days?

What are some ways you've learned to fight against anxiety and worry through these devotions?

How have you learned to focus your thoughts on God and His character when difficulties come?

display |

Listen to the song, "Fighting Words" by Ellie Holcomb, and commit to fighting the enemy's lies with God's truth.

> Thank God for all the ways He has grown you and given you peace as you've studied His Word over the last 30 days. Ask Him to bring to mind someone in your life who might be struggling with anxiety and fear.

Give them a copy of this book, and offer to walk through the devotions with them. Just as you find rest in Christ in the midst of your anxiety and fear, encourage others to do the same.

WHEN I AM AFRAID,

I will trust in you.

PSALM 56:3

Peace

display
challenges

Look back over each day
and find the challenges in
the Display section.
Write down any challenges
(or action steps) you took.

how did i fulfill them?

Write about how you followed through with each of the challenges on the previous page. Draw lines or arrows to connect your responses to the corresponding challenge.

resources

books

- *Fear and Faith: Finding the Peace Your Heart Craves* by Trillia Newbell
- *Anxious for Nothing* by Max Lucado
- *Afraid of All the Things* by Scarlet Hiltibidal
- *Rhythms of Renewal* by Rebekah Lyons
- *So Long Insecurity* by Beth Moore
- *God is Able* by Priscilla Shirer

articles and blogs

Check out these articles for more about Christians and anxiety.

- "Where Is God When Your Worst Fears Come True?" by Trillia Newbell
  (Today's Christian Woman, 2015)
- "When I Feel Afraid" by Leeann Stiles
  (The Gospel Coalition [TGC], 2014)
- "3 Ways Technology Makes Us Anxious" by Shelby Abbott
  (TGC, 2016)
- "Ask TGC: Is Anxiety a Sin?" by Joe Carter
  (TGC, 2019)
- "Scripture-Prayers for Taking Courage and Forsaking Fear" by Beth Moore
  (The LPM Blog, 2020)

videos and podcasts

- "I'm Not Anxious, I'm C.A.L.M." by The Proverbs 31 Ministries Podcast
- "Dr. Tony Evans - Overcoming Anxiety Strongholds | Part 1 - March 30, 2017" by Tony Evans - Radio (Youtube)
- "How to Overcome Fear in Your Life" by Better Together TV (Youtube)

find a counselor

Always, always talk with your parents if you're struggling. If you want to talk to a counselor or if your parents have approached you about doing so, these tools can help.

This list is certainly not exhaustive, but you and your parents can do the following to help you find a solid, biblical counselor.

- Check with your church first to see if they have qualified counselors on-site or have a list of recommended counselors to refer you to.

- Use a reputable search site to find a Christian counselor near you. These sites provide a search-by-location feature, but it's still a good idea to go through your results and make sure the counselor has experience with anxiety/anxiety disorders. These two sites are good places to start.

  - The Christian Counselor's Network (powered by Focus on the Family)

  - Christian Care Connect (powered by the American Association of Christian Counselors)

notes

notes

sources

1. Trillia Newbell, *Fear and Faith: Finding the Peace Your Heart Craves* (Chicago, IL: Moody Publishers, 2015), 16.
2. Max Lucado, *Anxious for Nothing: Finding Calm in A Chaotic World* (Nashville, TN: Thomas Nelson, 2017), 8.
3. Scarlet Hiltibidal, *Afraid of All the Things* (Nashville, TN: B&H Publishing Group, 2019).
4. Chrystal Hurst, "#055 - A Chat with Priscilla Shirer," Chrystal Evans Hurst, December 5, 2016, https://chrystalevanshurst.com/055-a-chat-with-priscilla-shirer/.
5. Rebekah Lyons, *Rhythms of Renewal* (Grand Rapids, MI: Zondervan), 151.
6. Jasmine Holmes, "Q & A: Jackie Hill Perry on 'Bending Myself to Jesus'," ChristianityToday.com (CT Women, May 24, 2018), https://www.christianitytoday.com/ct/2018/may-web-only/q-and-jackie-hill-perry-bending-myself-to-jesus-rap.html.
7. Dr. Gardneer C. Taylor, *Faith in the Fire* (New York: SmileyBooks, 2011), 86.
8. "Anxiety: Stop Negative Thoughts," Anxiety: Stop Negative Thoughts | Michigan Medicine, accessed August 18, 2020, https://www.uofmhealth.org/health-library/uf9897.
9. Adapted from Kathleen Smith, "Managing Test Anxiety: How to Cope and Perform Better," Psycom.net - Mental Health Treatment Resource Since 1986, April 11, 2019, https://www.psycom.net/managing-test-anxiety/; Adapted from "Generalized Anxiety Disorder 7-Item (GAD-7)," National HIV Curriculum, accessed August 17, 2020, https://www.hiv.uw.edu/page/mental-health-screening/gad-7.
9. "C. S. Lewis Daily," accessed July 22, 2020, https://www.biblegateway.com/devotionals/cs-lewis-daily/2018/04/13.
10. "G1515 - Eirēnē - Strong's Greek Lexicon (KJV)," Blue Letter Bible, accessed August 17, 2020, https://www.blueletterbible.org/lang/lexicon/lexicon.cfm?Strongs=G1515.